Some Like It Hot!

Yellowstone's Favorite Geysers, Hot Springs, and Fumaroles,
with Personal Accounts by Early Explorers

Susan M. Neider

RIVERBEND
PUBLISHING

Other titles by Susan M. Neider
Color Country: Touring the Colorado Plateau
High Country: Touring the Colorado Rockies
Golden Country: Touring Scenic California
Wild Yosemite: Personal Accounts of Adventure, Discovery, and Nature

Some Like It Hot!
Copyright © 2009 by Susan M. Neider

Published by Riverbend Publishing, Helena, Montana

ISBN 13: 978-1-60639-006-1
ISBN 10: 1-60639-006-6

Printed in South Korea

3 4 5 6 7 8 9 0 SI 15 14 13

Design by DD Dowden

RIVERBEND PUBLISHING
P.O. Box 5833
Helena, MT 59604
1-866-787-2363

www.riverbendpublishing.com

Emerald Pool ▶

To our days in Yellowstone remembered

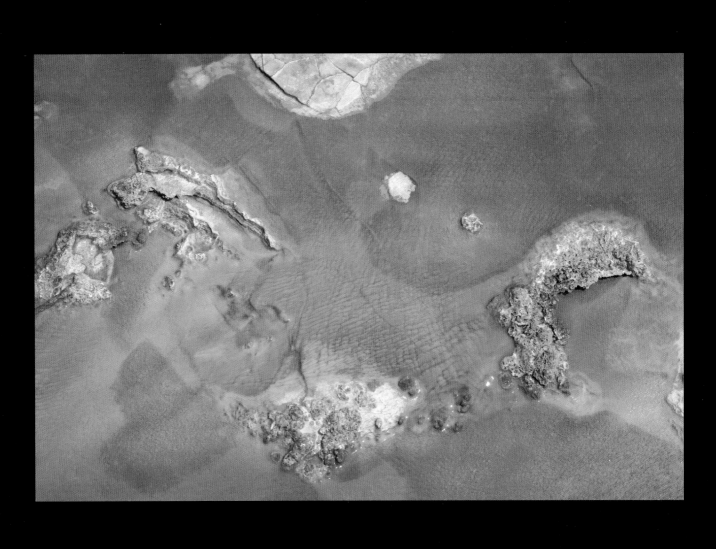

CONTENTS

Grand Geyser mud ◄

Abyss Pool and Yellowstone Lake ▲

Abyss Pool's "ultramarine hue of the transparent depth
in the bright sunlight was the most dazzlingly beautiful
sight I have ever beheld."

—F.V. HAYDEN, *PRELIMINARY REPORTS*, 1871

PREFACE

With only a couple of exceptions, I have had the good fortune to photograph every national park and monument in the American west, and then, of course, Yellowstone, our first national park. Add to that list most of the numerous state parks and scenic places along the way. I'd estimate this amounts to roughly 60,000 car miles and as many firings of the shutter, over ten years, traveling about four weeks a year.

It's hard to beat the breathtaking scenery of southern Utah and places like Sequoia and Yosemite, but I have had more fun in Yellowstone than in all those other parks combined. It's dynamic, it's elusive, it's chance, it's varied, and surprisingly, the thermal features are largely ignored as subjects of great beauty. Photographers hunt the wildlife but walk right by gems like Emerald Pool.

To be honest, Yellowstone is not easy to photograph, but I have tried to find a way to make it so. A polarizing filter is essential. It saturates color on wet surfaces and helps to underexpose the scene slightly so highlight detail isn't lost. There's so much light in the basins that a tripod isn't usually necessary. In fact, it slows me down, costing valuable time to recompose between geyser bursts and fast-moving steam skimming across the pools. I'd recommend using an image-stabilized lens instead. I always take a moment to consider exposures carefully because the camera's meter is easily fooled by dark pine forests in the background or blinding white limestone everywhere else. I shoot often and abundantly, and while I allow myself a certain amount of chimping, I make it a point not to edit my images until I am out of the park and back at my desk.

Yellowstone National Park is neatly organized by region. Wide, sturdy boardwalks thread through the thermal features, so it's impossible to get lost. The largest region is the Upper Geyser Basin surrounding Old Faithful, where I was able to shoot all the important geysers and hot springs on a walk of about three miles. In most regions, the park supplies excellent, self-guiding maps, which can be borrowed or purchased for 50 cents. These are worth collecting even if only as a record of the imaginative names of the features, too numerous to remember while working. Bathrooms are available throughout the park. Snacks and water are not. I've never been unexpectedly soaked by either geyser spray or rain while in Yellowstone. However it's a good precaution to bring protective covering for your gear. The great danger is the acidic content of the water and steam, which will etch your glass in no time. One learns this the hard way. I keep on hand a polarizer for use only in the geyser basins, and just accept the fact that the coating is spattered with acid marks.

Yellowstone hides other more serious dangers. In 2007, I witnessed a huge grizzly emerge from seemingly nowhere and scatter the crowds at Fountain Paint Pot. More obviously, bison in rut are thunderous and unswerving. Instinct and intellect don't always agree. That inviting pool of blue, refreshing to imagine, is actually boiling water contained in a crater with precariously thin crust. For reasons of personal safety and park preservation, it is critical that all visitors obey regulations and stay on the boardwalks.

Waiting for a geyser to erupt takes patience and often a lot of standing around; waiting for several to erupt can occupy an entire day. Serious geyser gazers wear comfortable shoes and adequate clothing, and often carry a portable chair, and of course, a watch. Many geysers have natural "indicators" that signal when an eruption is imminent, and knowing about them helps immeasurably in reducing the guesswork. By comparison, photographing hot springs is more leisurely and creative. The primary challenges there are composition and lighting, and the presence or absence of steam. When trying to capture mud exploding from a fumarole, I rely on the belief that the patron saint of photography is Chance.

Author in Porcelain Basin ▲

For all its photographic allure, Yellowstone National Park and the surrounding towns are not equipped to serve the needs of the unprepared photographer. I bring along everything that I can imagine needing, although I get most of my work done with only a 24-105mm lens; the rest is for just in case. Here's the list: Canon 5D body, three Canon L-series zoom lenses covering 20mm to 200mm, lens hoods, polarizing filter, three 4GB CF cards, three batteries and two chargers, Epson P-4000 multimedia storage viewer and charger, Gitzo tripod, Arca Swiss ball head, Canon G9 outfit, cleaning supplies, and a power strip to make life easier back in the hotel room.

Some Like It Hot! is a portfolio of photographs of my favorite thermal features of Yellowstone. Additionally, I've added as captions excerpts from a great variety of the journals of early expedition members reacting and describing what they were seeing. These personal accounts are beautifully written and timeless, as one would expect from good minds when writing about a newly discovered wonder of nature. While this collection provides a well-organized overview of the major and most beautiful thermal features, it is not intended to be a guidebook to Yellowstone National Park. There are many fine titles for that purpose. Rather, it is my hope to usher you in to the very best places, and then set you free.

Susan M. Neider

INTRODUCTION

"It is a pleasure now to say a few words to you at the laying of the corner stone of the beautiful arch which is to mark the entrance to this park. Yellowstone Park is something absolutely unique in the world so far as I know. Nowhere else in any civilized country is there to be found such a tract of veritable wonderland made accessible to all visitors...."
—President Theodore Roosevelt, April 24, 1903

"Yellowstone...is a big, wholesome wilderness on the broad summit of the Rocky Mountains, favored with abundance of rain and snow, a place of fountains where the greatest of the American rivers take their rise. The central portion is a densely forested and comparatively level volcanic plateau with an average elevation of about eight thousand feet above the sea, surrounded by an imposing host of mountains belonging to the subordinate Gallatin, Wind River, Teton, Absaroka, and Snowy ranges. Unnumbered lakes shine in it, united by a famous band of streams that rush up out of hot lava beds, or fall from the frosty peaks in channels rocky and bare, mossy and bosky, to the main rivers, singing cheerily on through every difficulty, cunningly dividing and finding their way east and west to the two far-off seas.

"For the Benefit and Enjoyment of the People" ▲

"Beside the treasures common to most mountain regions that are wild and blessed with a kind climate, the park is full of exciting wonders. The wildest geysers in the world, in bright, triumphant bands, are dancing and singing in it amid thousands of boiling springs, beautiful and awful, their basins arrayed in gorgeous colors like gigantic flowers; and hot paint pots, mud springs, mud volcanoes, mush and broth caldrons whose contents are of every color and consistency, splash and heave and roar in bewildering abundance.... Therefore it is called Wonderland, and thousands of tourists and travelers stream into it every summer, and wander about in it enchanted.

"However orderly your excursions or aimless, again and again amid the calmest, stillest scenery you will be brought to a standstill, hushed and awe-stricken, before phenomena wholly new to you. Boiling springs and huge deep pools of purest green and azure water, thousands of them, are splashing and heaving in these high, cool mountains, as if a fierce furnace fire were burning beneath each one of them; and a hundred geysers, white torrents of boiling water and steam, like inverted waterfalls, are ever and anon rushing up out of the hot, black underworld. Some of these ponderous geyser columns are as large as sequoias, —five to sixty feet in diameter, one hundred and fifty to three hundred feet high, —and are sustained at this great height with tremendous energy for a few minutes, or perhaps nearly an hour, standing rigid and erect, hissing, throbbing, booming, as if thunderstorms were raging beneath their roots, their sides roughened or fluted like the furrowed boles of trees, their tops dissolving in feathery branches, while the irised spray, like misty bloom, is at times blown aside, revealing the massive shafts shining against a background of pine-covered hills. Some of them lean more or less, as if storm-bent, and instead of being round are flat or fan-shaped, issuing from irregular slits in silex pavements with radiate structure, the sunbeams sifting through them in ravishing splendor. Some are broad and round-headed like oaks; others are low and bunchy, branching near the ground like bushes; and a few are hollow in the centre like big daisies or water lilies. No frost cools them, snow never covers them nor lodges in their branches; winter and summer they welcome alike; all of them, of whatever form or size, faithfully rising and sinking in fairy rhythmic dance night and day, in all sorts of weather, at varying periods of minutes, hours, or weeks, growing up rapidly, uncontrollable as fate, tossing their pearly branches in the wind, bursting into bloom and vanishing like the frailest flowers, plants of which Nature raises hundreds or thousands of crops a year with no apparent exhaustion of the fiery soil.

".... We see Nature working with enthusiasm like a man, blowing her volcanic forges like a blacksmith blowing his smithy fires, shoving glaciers over the landscapes like a carpenter shoving his planes, clearing, ploughing, harrowing, irrigating, planting, and sowing broadcast like a farmer and gardener doing rough work and fine work, planting sequoias and pines, rosebushes and daisies; working in gems, filling every crack and hollow with them; distilling fine essences; painting plants and shells, clouds, mountains, all the earth and heavens, like an artist, ever working toward beauty higher and higher. Where may the mind find more stimulating, quickening pasturage? A thousand Yellowstone wonders are calling, "Look up and down and round about you!" And a multitude of still, small voices may be heard directing you to look through all this transient, shifting show of things called 'substantial' into the truly substantial, spiritual world whose forms flesh and wood, rock and water, air and sunshine, only veil and conceal, and to learn that here is heaven and the dwelling place of the angels.

"Now comes the gloaming. The alpenglow is fading into earthy, murky gloom, but do not let your town habits draw you away to the hotel. Stay on this good fire-mountain and spend the night among the stars. Watch their glorious bloom until the dawn, and get one more baptism of light. Then, with fresh heart, go down to your work, and whatever your fate, under whatever ignorance or knowledge you may afterward chance to suffer, you will remember these fine, wild views, and look back with joy to your wanderings in the blessed old Yellowstone Wonderland."

—JOHN MUIR, "THE YELLOWSTONE NATIONAL PARK," *THE ATLANTIC MONTHLY,* APRIL 1898

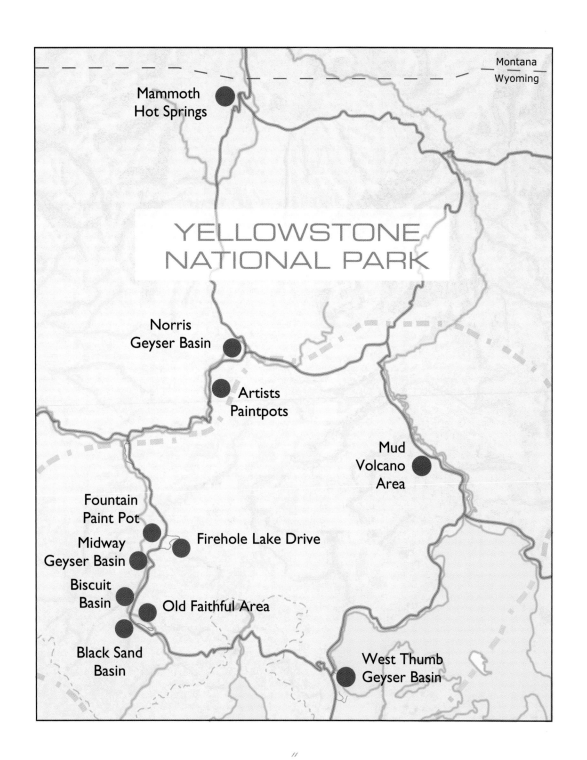

Montana
Wyoming

Mammoth
Hot Springs

YELLOWSTONE
NATIONAL PARK

Norris
Geyser Basin

Artists
Paintpots

Mud
Volcano
Area

Fountain
Paint Pot

Firehole Lake Drive

Midway
Geyser Basin

Biscuit
Basin

Old Faithful Area

Black Sand
Basin

West Thumb
Geyser Basin

TALLEST GEYSERS
IN YELLOWSTONE

200 feet or higher   Frequency
Steamboat in Norris (250'-386')   rare
Giant in Upper (150'-275')   infrequent
Great Fountain in Lower (10'-250')   8 to 17 hours

150 feet or higher:
Beehive in Upper (150'-200')   13 hours to days
Grand in Upper (150'-200')   8 to 12 hours
Giantess in Upper (100'-200')   infrequent
Splendid in Upper (50'-218')   rare
Old Faithful in Upper (106'-184')   60 to 127 minutes

100 feet or higher:
Daisy in Upper (75'-150')   85 to 240 minutes
Fan in Upper (100'-125')   often irregular; currently 3 to 5 days
Ledge in Norris (30'-125')   rare
Twin in West Thumb (60'-120')   dormant

50 feet or higher:
Castle in Upper (40'-100')   13 to 15 hours
Lion Geyser in Upper (30'-98')   1 to 1.5 hours
Riverside in Upper (75')   5.5 to 8.5 hours
Echinus in Norris (20'-75')   rare

ARTISTS PAINTPOTS

Artists
Paintpots ◄

Mineral Pool ▲

Mud burst ◀

In spring and early summer, paintpot mud is thin and watery, so the pots boil vigorously. By late summer, the mud thickens and is forced into giant bubbles and unusual midair shapes by escaping steam and gases.

Mud burst ▶

Gibbon Falls, south of Artists Paintpots ▶

"The road gradually narrowed and we entered the Gibbon Canyon. This rocky defile is about six miles in length, and in some places the cliffs are so close to the Gibbon River, which flows through the canyon, that there is scarcely room for the road. The Gibbon Falls is a beautiful cascade, and the rippling water coursing over the gentle incline forms a beautiful picture. On past the falls to the northward are numerous small springs with a strong sulphuric odor, some on one side of the river and some on the other. The only spring of importance is the 'Beryl.' It is one of the largest in the Park, and is quite near the roadside. The water is constantly boiling, and great quantities of hissing steam escape from it. The overflow from the rim of the spring runs across the roadway, and, although boiling hot, our horses did not hesitate an instant, but walked right through it."

—EDWARD S. PARKINSON, *WONDERLAND; OR, TWELVE WEEKS IN AND OUT OF THE UNITED STATES*, 1894

Beryl Spring, south of Artists Paintpots ▼

BISCUIT BASIN

"The variously tinted sinter and travertine formations, outspread like pavements over large areas of the geyser valleys, lining the spring basins and throats of the craters, and forming beautiful coral-like rims and curbs about them, always excite admiring attention; so also does the play of the waters from which they are deposited. The various minerals in them are rich in fine colors, and these are greatly heightened by a smooth, silky growth of brilliantly colored confervæ, which lines many of the pools and channels and terraces. No bed of flower-bloom is more exquisite than these myriads of minute plants, visible only in mass, growing in the hot waters."

—John Muir, "The Yellowstone National Park," *The Atlantic Monthly,* April 1898

Jewel Geyser ◄
Biscuit Basin ▼

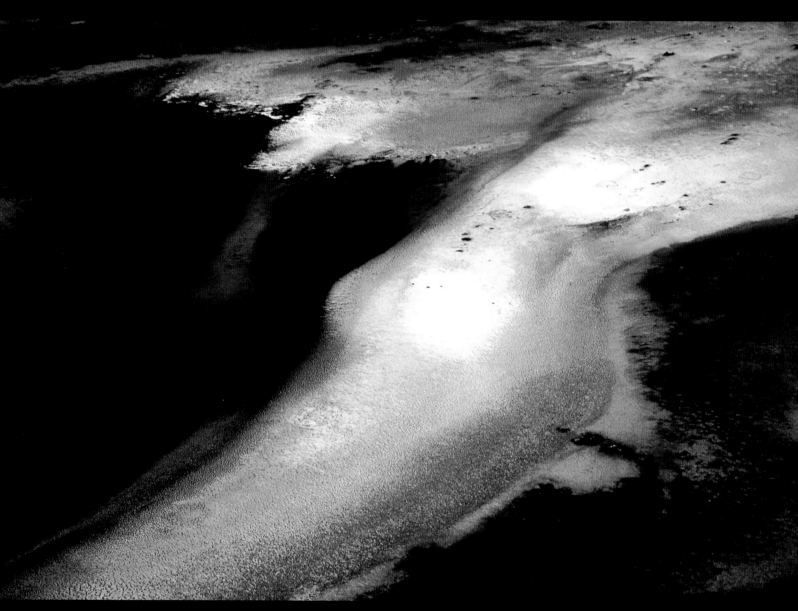

Sand ▲
Wall Pool and Black Opal Spring ▶

Shell Spring ▲
Sapphire Pool and thermophiles ▶

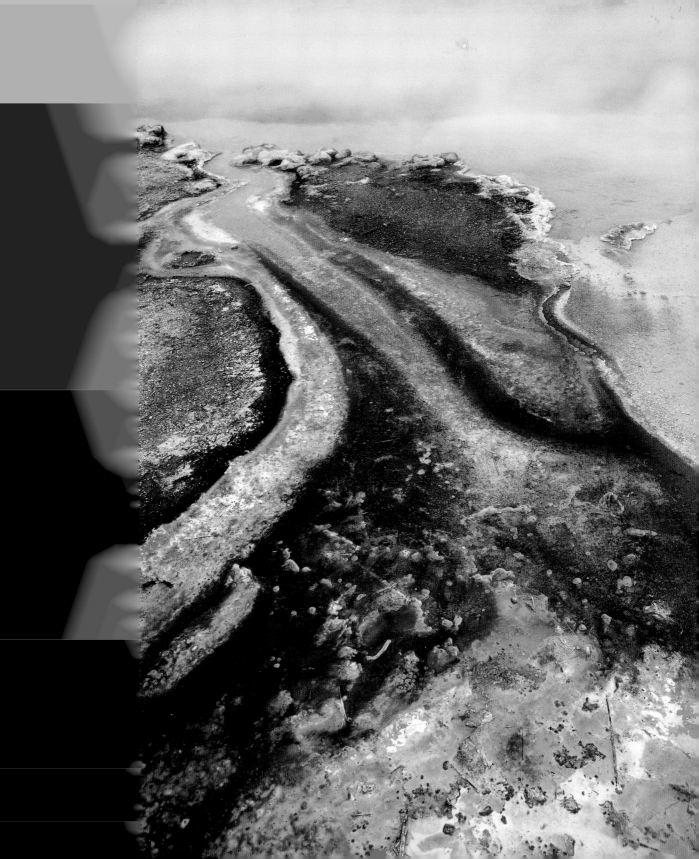

Thermophiles ▲
Thermophiles ▶

Green Spring ▲
Black Sand Basin boardwalk ▶

BLACK SAND BASIN

"Our plan was to cross the range in a northwesterly direction, find the Madison River, and follow it down to civilization. Twelve miles [from Yellowstone Lake, *ed.*] brought us to a small triangular-shaped lake [Shoshone Lake, *ed.*], about eight miles long, deeply set among the hills. We kept on in a northwesterly direction, as near as the rugged nature of the country would permit; and on the third day came to a small irregularly shaped valley, some six miles across in the widest place, from every part of which great clouds of steam arose. From descriptions which we had had of this valley, from persons who had previously visited it, we recognized it as the place known as 'Burnt Hole,' 'Death Valley' [Upper Geyser Basin, *ed.*]. The Madison River [Iron Creek of the Firehole River, *ed.*] flows through it, and from the general contour of the country we knew that it headed in the lake which we passed two days ago, only twelve miles from the Yellowstone [River, *ed.*]. We descended into the valley, and found that the springs had the same general characteristics as those I have already described, although some of them were much larger and discharged a vast amount of water. One of them, at a little distance, attracted our attention by the immense amount of steam it threw off; and upon approaching it we found it to be an intermittent geyser in active operation. The hole through which the water was discharged was ten feet in diameter, and was situated in the centre of a large circular shallow basin, into which the water fell.... At that moment the escaping steam was causing the water to boil up in a fountain five or six feet high. It stopped in an instant, and commenced settling down—twenty, thirty, forty feet —until we concluded that the bottom had fallen out; but the next instant, without any warning, it came rushing up and shot into the air at least eighty feet.... It continued to spout at intervals of a few minutes, for some time; but finally subsided, and was quiet during the remainder of the time we stayed in the vicinity."

—FOLSOM-COOK-PETERSON EXPEDITION, 1869

Cliff Geyser and Iron Spring Creek ▲ [left]

"On the bank of Iron [Spring, *ed.*] Creek and near a sharp point in the stream not far from the Emerald, is situated Cliff Geyser, a singularly picturesque basin. It has built up from the stream a semicircular wall several feet above high-water level, the corrugated outer rim being produced during the building up of the sinter by an incessant downflow of water. According to Mr. Weed, 'the two vents of Cliff Geyser seem built up along the same fissure, though their activity is slightly different. The west vent bubbles quietly and the basin about it is lined with light gold algae. The main vent is undoubtedly a fissure one to three feet wide and five feet long, the hole being five feet below the surface of the pool.'" —Arnold Hague, assistant to Walter Weed, 1911

Cliff Geyser ▲ [right]

"I have also to add one new geyser to those reported in the Upper Basin. It is situated in the Emerald Group [Black Sand Basin, *ed.*]. I have named it the Cliff Geyser, as it lies so close under the abrupt wall which skirts the west bank of Iron [Spring, *ed.*] Creek."—Arnold Hague, assistant to Walter Weed, 1884

Opalescent Pool ▲

Opalescent Pool "revealed an opalescent azure as lovely as the sky above." — Naturalist Herbert Lystrup, 1957

Rainbow Pool ▲

Emerald Pool ▲

"Deep basin, fifty feet long and twenty wide. The lining of the basin is a chocolate colored deposit, which assumes a brown tint when dry. A low rim of scalloped geyserite surrounds the spring, but is badly broken in places.…

The water is clear and in quiet ebullition, tho' the spring evidently overflows, at times, as the outer basin and the channel are both coated with fresh and moist geyserite."
—WALTER WEED, *NOTEBOOK VOLUME III*, 1883

Sunset Lake ▲

"Near the mouth of the stream, and on the west side, is a lake of bluestone water, one hundred feet in diameter, with steam evolving from its waters, which flow over a low rim in every direction down the slopes depositing a yellow bed, which is now many feet in thickness."

—G.C. Doane of the General H.D. Washburn-Langford-Doane Expedition, 1870

Sunset Lake ▲

Sunset Lake "is a saucer-like depression, deep in the center and filled with hot water, receiving its supply from the vents near the center, and as the outer edge is shallow, the surplus water readily falls off toward the stream. From this pool volumes of steam are constantly rising, and the accompanying displays of red and yellow tints upon the surface is only surpassed by Prismatic Lake [Grand Prismatic Spring, *ed.*] in Excelsior Basin [Midway Geyser Basin, *ed.*]."

—ARNOLD HAGUE, ASSISTANT TO WALTER WEED, 1911

FIREHOLE LAKE DRIVE
in LOWER GEYSER BASIN

"*In the angle of the woods at the mouth of the creek are several large bluestone springs, some flowing, others quiescent. Whole trees fallen in the craters of these are incrusted with a white, calcareous deposit, and gradually turn to stone; leaves, pine cones, grasshoppers, and twigs, are also thus incrusted in the most delicate manner.*"
—G.C. Doane of the General H.D. Washburn-Langford-Doane Expedition, 1870

White Dome Geyser ◄
Firehole Spring ▼

Great Fountain Geyser ▲

"Our attention was at once attracted by water and steam escaping, or being thrown up from an opening.... Soon this geyser was in full play. The setting sun shining into the spray and steam drifting toward the mountains, gave it the appearance of burnished gold, a wonderful sight. We could not contain our enthusiasm: with one accord we all took off our hats and yelled with all our might."

—Folsom-Cook-Peterson Expedition, 1869

FOUNTAIN PAINT POT AREA
in LOWER GEYSER BASIN

"*These 'paint-pots' are large vats of boiling mud which are continually sputtering and throwing particles of mud in every direction. Some of the mud had a pinkish color and the rest shades off to pure white.*"

—EDWARD S. PARKINSON, *WONDERLAND; OR, TWELVE WEEKS IN AND OUT OF THE UNITED STATES*, 1894

Fountain Paint Pot ▼

Clepsydra
and Spasm
Geysers ▶

Fountain Paint Pot fumarole ▲

"These valleys at the heads of the great rivers may be regarded as laboratories and kitchens, in which, amid a thousand retorts and pots, we may see Nature at work as chemist or cook, cunningly compounding an infinite variety of mineral messes; cooking whole mountains; boiling and steaming flinty rocks to smooth paste and mush, —yellow, brown, red, pink, lavender, gray, and creamy white, —making the most beautiful mud in the world; and distilling the most ethereal essences. Many of these pots and caldrons have been boiling thousands of years. Pots of sulphurous mush, stringy and lumpy, and pots of broth as black as ink, are tossed and stirred with constant care, and thin transparent essences, too pure and fine to be called water, are kept simmering gently in beautiful sinter cups and bowls that grow ever more beautiful the longer they are used. In some of the spring basins, the waters, though still warm, are perfectly calm, and shine blandly in a sod of overleaning grass and flowers, as if they were thoroughly cooked at last, and set aside to settle and cool. Others are wildly boiling over as if running to waste, thousands of tons of the precious liquids being thrown into the air to fall in scalding floods on the clean coral floor of the establishment, keeping onlookers at a distance. Instead of holding limpid pale green or azure water, other pots and craters are filled with scalding mud, which is tossed up from three or four feet to thirty feet, in sticky, rank-smelling masses, with gasping, belching, thudding sounds, plastering the branches of neighboring trees; every flask, retort, hot spring, and geyser has something special in it, no two being the same in temperature, color, or composition."

—John Muir, "The Yellowstone National Park," *The Atlantic Monthly*, April 1898

Fountain Geyser ▶

"While watching for some indication of the approaching eruption of the Fountain Geyser, a few bubbles were noticed coming up from the depths of the pool, and then there was a lively scampering to get out of the way of any stray sprays of hot water that might reach the spectators. In a few moments the water shot up for a distance of about twenty feet, which was followed by one of those magnificent displays of the workings of Nature which is only to be witnessed in the Yellowstone Park. We stood for fully ten minutes watching the water as it was thrown to a height of from twenty to twenty-five feet, although sometimes jets would be forced to twice or three times that height."

—EDWARD S. PARKINSON,
WONDERLAND; OR, TWELVE WEEKS IN AND OUT OF THE UNITED STATES, 1894

Silex Spring ▲

Lower Geyser Basin ▲

"Early in the afternoon we crossed the mountain and our eyes for the first time beheld 'Wonderland.' Vast columns of steam were ascending from the many geysers and boiling springs which abound in the valley...."

—EDWARD S. PARKINSON, *WONDERLAND; OR, TWELVE WEEKS IN AND OUT OF THE UNITED STATES,* 1894

Trees ◄

"In many localities there were large groups of standing trees in these marshes, dead and denuded of bark to the height of three feet, their bare trunks being a snowy whiteness and fast turning to stone. These were always found in places where hot water flowed down at some period from geysers above. They presented, with their deadened tops and bare and white-washed stumps, a very singular appearance."
—G.C. Doane of the General H.D. Washburn-Langford-Doane Expedition, 1870

Lodgepole pine ►

"The so-called geyser basins…are mostly open valleys on the central plateau that were eroded by glaciers after the greater volcanic fires had ceased to burn. Looking down over the forests as you approach them from the surrounding heights, you see a multitude of white columns, broad, reeking masses, and irregular jets and puffs of misty vapor ascending from the bottom of the valley, or entangled like smoke among the neighboring trees, suggesting the factories of some busy town or the campfires of an army. These mark the position of each mush pot, paint pot, hot spring, and geyser, or gusher, as the Icelandic word means. And when you saunter into the midst of them over the bright sinter pavements, and see how pure and white and pearly gray they are in the shade of the mountains, and how radiant in the sunshine, you are fairly enchanted. So numerous they are and varied, Nature seems to have gathered them from all the world as specimens of her rarest fountains, to show in one place what she can do."
—John Muir, "The Yellowstone National Park," *The Atlantic Monthly*, April 1898

Canary Spring ▲

MAMMOTH HOT SPRINGS

"As the Mammoth Hot Springs basin is destines to become the focal point for all tourists in the Yellowstone Park, a sketch of the topography, extent, and appearance of the springs and terraces may be of some interest at this time….The remarkable calcareous deposit of lime, magnesia, sulphur, and other precipitates left by the action and evaporation of the Hot Springs extends down and has filled up a considerable part of this basin from Sepulchre Mountain to the river, and I judge its length to be certainly not less than three miles and a half. It would be wild for any one not a scientist to express an opinion as to the length of time required to produce this gigantic formation. With a scientist even much would be conjectural. The foothills and mounds have been enveloped in the chalky deposit and the dells and depressions leveled up by it to a great extent. The result is the erection of some five or six main terraces, varying from perhaps one hundred fifty to fifty feet in elevation above each other. The accretion of chemicals has gone slowly onward for centuries until on some of the terraces pine and cedar trees, forty to seventy-five feet in height, have been submerged so that now only their topmost branches, withered and white, crop out above the surface. In many places undoubtedly the trees have been completely overwhelmed. The lofty terraces spoken of are seamed and ridged and divided up into smaller terraces, so that that the ascent of the bluffs at their faces can only be made by climbing on zigzag paths. Viewed from in front the terraces look much like hillsides, one behind another, covered with snow.

In many places they are streaked down their faces with various shades of ochre, brown, gray-yellow, and bluish white. The prevailing color is a dingy white, set off at irregular intervals by bands of the purest snowy hue, and the other tints I have named. Here and there all over 'the formation,' as the terraces are called here, cedar and other trees of the fir family have taken root and given rise to wonder as to the source of their sustenance….

"In the foreground are two great columns built by now defunct springs —one forty-seven feet high and twelve feet in diameter, known as the Liberty Cap, and the other, not so large, called Devil's Thumb. Directly behind these columns the terraces are piled up one above the other in steep cliffs, and the ascent is no longer easy. On the plateaus of all of these terraces there [are, *ed.*] active hot springs, the greatest display being made above the lofty red cliff called the Pulpit Terraces. Standing on some one of the snowy knobs that arise near the little chalky gorge called Antony's Gate, and looking down on these crystal-clear pools the eye and the senses are charmed by the soft beauty, the varied outlines, and the exquisite blending of color which they present. I had seen some of Moran's paintings of these hot pools and always had a suspicion that he had gone just a little wild in his appetite for color effect. Now that I have seen the springs I know that he stopped short of the reality."

— "The Yellowstone Park: Wonders of the Mammoth Hot Springs Basin," *The New York Times,* July 22, 1883

Canary Spring ◄
Mammoth Hot Springs ▲

Liberty Cap ▶

"At the base of the terraces stands an extinct cone known as the Liberty Cap, about fifty feet in height and twenty feet in diameter at the base. It is some distance from the mountain, and from the appearance of the overlapping layers of carbonate of lime one would think it had no proper connection with the mountain."

—EDWARD S. PARKINSON,
WONDERLAND; OR, TWELVE WEEKS IN AND OUT OF THE UNITED STATES, 1894

Orange Spring Mound ▲

Palette Spring ▶
Palette Spring ▼

Travertine terrace ▲

"Or, as in the case of the Mammoth Hot Springs, at the north end of the park, where the building waters issue from the side of a steep hill, the deposits form a succession of higher and broader terraces of white travertine tinged with purple, …draped in front with clustering stalactites, each terrace having a pool of indescribably beautiful water upon it in a basin with a raised rim that glistens with confervæ, —the whole, when viewed at a distance of a mile or two, looking like a broad, massive cascade pouring over shelving rocks in snowy purpled foam. The stones of this divine masonry, invisible particles of lime or silex, mined in quarries no eye has seen, go to their appointed places in gentle, tinkling, transparent currents or through the dashing turmoil of floods, as surely guided as the sap of plants streaming into bole and branch, leaf and flower. And thus from century to century this beauty-work has gone on and is going on."

—John Muir, "The Yellowstone National Park," *The Atlantic Monthly*, April 1898

Upper Terrace and the Absaroka Range ▲

MIDWAY GEYSER BASIN

"Moving down the stream on the north side, past springs and small geysers of every variety, for a distance of three miles, we then traversed a valley five miles in length, swampy in many places, and in others much obstructed by fallen timber. Thermal springs were scattered along the whole route, but none large enough to be remarkable here. In eight miles we came to an enormous bluestone spring, nearly circular in form, four hundred fifty yards in circumference, and of unfathomable depth, boiling hot, and with clouds of steam evolving from its surface. It has built up a hill fifty feet above the general level, and covering about one hundred acres with a calcareous bed. The margin of the great basin is bounded by a rim thirty feet back from the brink of the crater, and elevated a few inches. The waters overflow in every direction, keeping the long slopes constantly wet. The deposits are of variegated colors—a circumstance not before remarked in any springs of this class; the water boils up slightly in many places far out in the basin, but steadily, and with no indication of violent or periodic action. The steam rising is evolved from the surface of the water, and does not escape through it from beneath. The margin of this lake is a hundred and fifty yards from the [Firehole, *ed*.] river, which has cut away its deposit to a bluff bank, forty-six feet in height, at that distance. Between this bluff and the basin, but at a lower level, by twenty feet, is a geyser with a basin fifty feet in diameter, and playing a strong jet from the center to the height of twenty feet. Just beyond this, and at a different level still, are several smaller geysers, and a bluestone spring [Excelsior Geyser, *ed*.] seventy feet in diameter. Flowing from these latter over the bank into the river are five streams of boiling water, either one large enough to run an ordinary gristmill. These steaming cataracts are among the most beautiful we have witnessed on the trip."

—G.C. Doane of the General H.D. Washburn-Langford-Doane Expedition, 1870

Midway Geyser Basin ◄
Turquoise Pool runoff ►

Excelsior Geyser ▲

"Four or five miles below the [Upper, *ed.*] geyser basin, on the west side of the Firehole, were four hot lakes. They were similar to the clear, pale-violet pools which we saw above…but were very much larger. Three of the party paced around the largest one, making the circumference four hundred and fifty paces. It looked very deep. The sides of the whitest subsilica converged at an angle of about forty-five degrees. It was full to the brim, and a track, about twenty feet wide all around it, was covered with two inches of water, which was so hot that it almost scalded our feet, through heavy boots. Before our pacers got all the way round, they stepped not only very high, but in quite a lively, animated style. Beyond the track of water which circled the lake, the ground, covered with subsilica, sloped away gradually on all sides. Immense volumes of steam rose from all these lakes, and first attracted our attention to them. So much hot water flowed from them that the Firehole was tempered for several miles below. We found no fish anywhere in the Firehole, though after its junction with the Madison they were quite plentiful."

—WALTER TRUMBALL, *OVERLAND MONTHLY,* JUNE 1871

Excelsior Geyser ◄

"We bid farewell to the Geysers, little dreaming there were more beyond. Five miles beyond Burnt Hole [Upper Geyser Basin, *ed.*] we found the 'Lake of Fire and Brimstone.' In the valley we found a lake measuring four hundred and fifty yards in diameter, gently overflowing, that had built itself up by deposit of white substrata, at least fifty feet above the plain. This body of water was steaming hot. Below this was a similar spring, but of smaller dimensions while between the two, and apparently having no connection with either, was a spring of enormous volume flowing into the Madison [Firehole River, *ed.*], and is undoubtedly the spring which Bridger has been laughed at so much about, as heating the Madison for two miles below."

—GENERAL H.D. WASHBURN, *EXPLORATIONS IN A NEW AND WONDERFUL COUNTRY,* 1870

Firehole River ▲

"Near the Prismatic Spring is the great Excelsior Geyser, which is said to throw a column of boiling water sixty to seventy feet in diameter to a height of from fifty to three hundred feet, at irregular periods. This is the greatest of all the geysers yet discovered anywhere. The Firehole River, which sweeps past it, is, at ordinary stages, a stream about one hundred yards wide and three feet deep; but when the geyser is in eruption, so great is the quantity of water discharged that the volume of the river is doubled, and it is rendered too hot and rapid to be forded."

—JOHN MUIR, "THE YELLOWSTONE NATIONAL PARK," *THE ATLANTIC MONTHLY,* APRIL 1898

Firehole River ▼

"The overflow from the spring pours over the slope in small channels, or spreads over broad surfaces, where the evaporation of the water has deposited a crust of a marvelous combination of tints. The coloring is very vivid, and of many shades, from bright scarlet to delicate rose, mingled with bright and creamy yellows, and vivid green from the minute vegetation."

—F.V. HAYDEN, *THE YELLOWSTONE NATIONAL PARK, AND THE MOUNTAIN REGIONS OF PORTIONS OF IDAHO, NEVADA, COLORADO, AND UTAH,* 1876

Grand Prismatic Spring ▲

"This section is known as 'Hell's Half Acre,' [Rudyard Kipling, 1889, *ed.*] from the great number of boiling springs in the vicinity. Prismatic lake [Grand Prismatic Spring, *ed.*] is perhaps a couple of hundred yards west from the 'Excelsior,' and receives its name from the many colors visible on its surface. The water in the centre of the lake is deep blue, gradually shading off to green. When the shallower portion of the lake is reached it assumes a yellow color, which deepens to a distinct orange. The formation around the rim of the basin is a brilliant red. The constantly rising volumes of steam are tinged with the colors that are so prominent in the pool, and form one of the most pleasing effects of the Park."

—EDWARD S. PARKINSON, *WONDERLAND; OR, TWELVE WEEKS IN AND OUT OF THE UNITED STATES,* 1894

Grand Prismatic Spring ▲

"The largest and one of the most wonderfully beautiful of the springs is the Prismatic…. With a circumference of three hundred yards, it is more like a lake than a spring. The water is pure deep blue in the centre, fading to green on the edges, and its basin and the slightly terraced pavement about it are astonishingly bright and varied in color. This one of the multitude of Yellowstone fountains is of itself object enough for a trip across the continent. No wonder that so many fine myths have originated in springs; that so many fountains were held sacred in the youth of the world, and had miraculous virtues ascribed to them. Even in these cold, doubting, questioning, scientific times many of the Yellowstone fountains seem able to work miracles."

—JOHN MUIR, "THE YELLOWSTONE NATIONAL PARK," *THE ATLANTIC MONTHLY*, APRIL 1898

Grand Prismatic Spring and storm ▲

"We followed up the Madison [Firehole River, *ed.*] five miles, and there found the most gigantic hot springs we had seen. They were situated along the riverbank, and discharged so much hot water that the river was blood-warm a quarter of a mile below. One of the springs was two hundred and fifty feet in diameter, and had every indication of spouting powerfully at times. The waters from the hot springs in this valley, if united, would form a large stream; and they increase the size of the *river* nearly one-half. Although we experienced no bad effects from passing through the 'Valley of Death,' yet we were not disposed to dispute the propriety of giving it that name. It seemed to be shunned by all animated nature. There were no fish in the river, no birds in the trees, no animals —not even a track —anywhere to be seen; although in one spring we saw the entire skeleton of a buffalo that had probably fallen in accidentally and been boiled down to soup."

—FOLSOM-COOK-PETERSON EXPEDITION, 1869

Turquoise Pool ▲

MUD VOLCANO AREA

"After spending one day at the [Yellowstone, *ed.*] falls we moved up the river. Above the falls there is but little current comparatively for several miles, and the country opens into a wide, open, treeless plain. About eight miles from the falls, and in this plain, we found three hills, or rather mountains, thrown up by volcanic agency, and consisting of scoria and a large admixture of brimstone. These hills are several hundred feet high, and evidently are now resting over what was once the crater of a volcano. A third of the way up on the side of one of these hills is a large sulphuric spring, twenty feet by twelve, filled with boiling water, and this water is thrown up from three to five feet. The basin of this spring is pure solid brimstone, as clear and bright as any brimstone of commerce. Quite a stream flows from the spring, and sulphur is found encrusting nearly everything. Near the base of the hills is a place containing about half an acre, but covered with springs of nearly every description, —yellow, green, blue and pink. Flowing from the base of the hill is a very strong spring of alum water —not only alum in solution, but crystallized. This place we called Crater Hill [Sulphur Spring, *ed.*], and as we passed over, the dull sound coming from our horses' feet as they struck, proved to us that it was not far through the crust. All over the hill were small fissures, giving out sulphurous vapors. The amount of brimstone in these hills is beyond belief.

"Passing over the plain we camped on the riverbank, near a series of mud springs [Mud Volcano Area, *ed.*]. Three of the largest were about ten feet over the top and had built up ten or twelve feet high. In the bottom of the crater thus [mud was, *ed.*] sputtering and splashing, as we have often seen in a pot of hasty pudding when nearly cooked. Near these we found a cave under the side of the mountain, from which was running a stream of clear but very hot water [Dragon's Mouth Spring, *ed.*]. At regular intervals the steam was puffing out. For some time we had been hearing a noise as of distant artillery, and soon we found the cause. Some distance above the level of the river we found the crater of a mud volcano [Mud Volcano, *ed.*], forty feet over at its mouth. It grew smaller until at the depth of thirty feet, when it again enlarged. At intervals a volume of mud and steam was thrown up with tremendous power and noise… A short time before our visit, mud had been thrown two or three hundred feet high, as shown by the trees in the vicinity. Not far from this we found our first geyser [Mud Geyser, *ed.*]. When discovered it was throwing water thirty or forty feet high. The crater was funnel-shaped, and seventy-five by thirty-five feet at its mouth. We stayed and watched it one day. Without warning it suddenly ceased to spout, and the water commenced sinking until it had gone down thirty feet or more. It then gradually commenced rising again, and three times during the day threw up water thirty or forty feet."

—GENERAL H.D. WASHBURN, *EXPLORATIONS IN A NEW AND WONDERFUL COUNTRY,* 1870

Lower Falls of the Yellowstone ◀

Churning Caldron ▶

Bacterial mat near
Churning Caldron ▼

"There being no good grass near Crater Hills [Sulphur Spring, *ed.*], after stopping a few hours to examine them we moved to a point on the Yellowstone about three miles above. Near this camp were several mineral springs, all hot, and many of them boiling. Most of them were ordinary, bubbling, spluttering mud-springs, but three of them were quite remarkable. Of these the first, or lowest down the river, is a cave-spring [Dragon's Mouth Spring, *ed.*], with an opening of ten feet in width by six in height, in solid rock, with an almost perfect, oval arch. The water is clear as crystal, of boiling heat, and a vitriolic taste. As you look into the cave, it has the appearance of an opening to a subterranean lake. A small, hot stream flows from it. The water is continually washing its ten or twelve feet of shore, like an agitated lake. The bright pebbles in the bottom, the clean sand, and the smooth, white, flat stones left in regular ripples on its margin, together with the green, mossy sides of the cave, and the musical monotones of the rippling waters, almost lead one to think it the entrance to an enchanted lake. A hundred yards above this spring, upon the side of a hill, was another entirely different in character. It was really a small volcano [Mud Volcano, *ed.*], throwing mud instead of lava. Intermittent thumps, like the discharge of artillery, could be heard, at intervals of from fifteen to thirty seconds, for the distance of a mile. At every pulsation, think, white clouds of steam came rolling out, and mud was thrown from the crater, gradually enlarging the mound, which surrounded it. While we were watching this spring the mud was only thrown over the rim of the crater, but from the clay clinging to the branches

of surrounding trees, especially on the upper side of the spring, it was evidently thrown, at times, to a height of two hundred feet. A circle, a hundred yards in diameter, was also well bespattered. Between the last-mentioned spring and the river is a boiling spring, a placid pond, a deep, dry funnel, or an active geyser, according to the time of one's visit. In the course of a day we saw it in all its protean shapes. When in its funnel form, one would not dream that, from the small opening in the bottom, twenty or thirty feet below, would come a power capable of filling with water the funnel, which at the top is thirty feet by forty, and then so agitating it that the water would be splashed to a height of from thirty to fifty feet. If one saw it when the waters were troubled, he would be scarcely less astonished to hear it give one convulsive throb, and then see it quietly settle down in a single instant to the smooth surface of a placid pool. When the waters retired we went into the funnel, and found it rough, efflorescent, and composed of rock and hardened sulphur. Though very different in character from the geysers afterward seen on the headwaters of the Madison River, and far less grand, this one was very peculiar, and we saw nothing resembling it during the rest of the trip."

—Walter Trumball, *Overland Monthly*, June 1871

Dragon's Mouth Spring ▶

Mud Volcano ▼

"On the slope of a small and steep wooded ravine is the crater of a mud volcano, thirty feet in diameter at the rim, which is elevated a few feet above the surface on the lower side, and bounded by the slope of the hill on the upper, converging, as it deepens, to the diameter of fifteen feet at the lowest visible point, about forty feet down. Heavy volumes of steam escape from this opening, ascending to the height of three hundred feet. From far down in the earth came a jarring sound, in regular beats of five seconds, with a concussion that shook the ground at two hundred yards distant. After each concussion came a splash of mud, as if thrown to a great height; sometimes it could be seen from the edge of the crater, but none was entirely ejected while we were there. Occasionally an explosion was heard like the bursting of heavy guns behind an embankment, and causing the earth to tremble for a mile around. These explosions were accompanied by a vast increase of the volumes of steam poured forth from the crater. This volcano has not been long in operation, as young pines, crushed flat to the earth under the rim of mud, were still alive at the tops. The amount of matter ejected was not great, considering the power of the volcano. The distances to which this mud has been thrown are truly astonishing. Directly above the crater rises a steep bank, a hundred feet in height, on the apex of which the tallest tree near is one hundred ten feet high. The topmost branches of this tree were loaded with mud two hundred feet above, and fifty feet latterly away from the crater. The ground and fallen trees nearby were splashed at a horizontal distance of two hundred feet. The trees below were either broken down, or their branches festooned with dry mud, which appeared in the tops of tree growing on the side hill from the same level with the crater, fifty feet in height, and at a distance of one hundred eighty feet from the volcano. The mud, to produce such effects, must have been thrown to a perpendicular elevation of at least three hundred feet.... It was with difficulty we could believe the evidence of our senses, and, only after the most careful measurements, could we realize the immensity of this wonderful phenomenon."

—G.C. Doane of the General H.D. Washburn-Langford-Doane Expedition, 1870

Mud Caldron ▲

Mud Geyser ▶

"A day and a half more brought the party to the Hot Sulphur and Mud Springs [Sulphur Spring, formerly called Crater Hills, *ed.*], sixty to seventy-five in number, of diameters varying from two to seventy feet. From scores of craters on the side of the mountain adjoining these springs, issue hot vapors, the edges of the craters being incrusted with pure sulphur. Six miles further on is the first geyser [Mud Geyser, *ed.*], which throws a column of water twenty feet in diameter in the height of thirty to thirty-five feet. Nearby is a volcano [Mud Volcano, *ed.*], which throws up mud from the bottom of its crater to the height of thirty feet or more, with explosions resembling distant discharges of cannon, the pulsations occurring at intervals of five seconds, and the explosions shaking the ground for a long distance. This volcano has evidently been in existence but a short time —a few months —as the newly grown grass was covered for nearly two hundred feet with the clayey mud that was thrown out at the first outbreak. The crater of this volcano is about thirty feet in diameter at its mouth, and is narrowed down to a diameter of fifteen feet at a depth of twenty feet from the top, and the surface of the mud down in the crater appeared, when for a few seconds it was in a quiescent state, to be about sixty feet below the mouth of the crater."

—N.P. Langford, "Interesting Data of the Trip, from Notes Furnished by Hon. N. P. Langford," *Helena Daily Herald*, September 26, 1870

Sulphur Caldron ▲

NORRIS GEYSER BASIN

"The Black Growler is located quite near the road, on top of the hill overlooking the entire basin. It takes its name from the peculiar growling noise caused by the great quantities of escaping steam and a black deposit in the vicinity. It is what might be called a steam geyser, as very little water is discharged from its crater."

—EDWARD S. PARKINSON, *WONDERLAND; OR, TWELVE WEEKS IN AND OUT OF THE UNITED STATES*, 1894

Crackling Lake ◄
Black Growler ▼

Colloidal Pool ▲

Whirligig Geyser algae ▶
Runoff ▼

Pinwheel Geyser ▲

Porcelain Basin ▲

Porcelain Basin ▲

"In these natural laboratories one needs stout faith to feel at ease. The ground sounds hollow underfoot, and the awful subterranean thunder shakes one's mind as the ground is shaken, especially at night in the pale moonlight, or when the sky is overcast with storm clouds. In the solemn gloom, the geysers, dimly visible, look like monstrous dancing ghosts, and their wild songs and the earthquake thunder replying to the storms overhead seem doubly terrible, as if divine government were at an end. But the trembling hills keep their places.

The sky clears, the rosy dawn is reassuring, and up comes the sun like a god, pouring his faithful beams across the mountains and forest, lighting each peak and tree and ghastly geyser alike, and shining into the eyes of the reeking springs, clothing them with rainbow light, and dissolving the seeming chaos of darkness into varied forms of harmony."

—John Muir, "The Yellowstone National Park,"
The Atlantic Monthly, April 1898

Steam ▲

"It was about noon when we got the first sight of the Norris Basin of geysers. It is a barren tract, and resembles an immense area recently swept by a terrific fire. From many places jets of steam are constantly rising, and here and there are to be seen quite a number of geysers....

This basin is supposed to be of more recent origin than any of the others in the Park, as there is an absence of cones around the craters of the geysers."

—EDWARD S. PARKINSON, *WONDERLAND; OR, TWELVE WEEKS IN AND OUT OF THE UNITED STATES,* 1894

Steamboat Geyser
fumes but seldom
erupts ◀

OLD FAITHFUL
and UPPER GEYSER BASIN

"The following day we traveled northwest, and soon reached the Firehole River. After passing by a fine cascade —which we stopped but a short time to examine —we forded the river, and camped about noon in the midst of the most wonderful geysers yet discovered in any country. The basin in which they were situated was over two miles long, and about a mile wide. It was nearly destitute of vegetation, but there were a few clumps of trees scattered through it, and in one place we found grass enough for our horses. The basin was chiefly on the west side of the river, but there was a narrow strip, with an average width of three hundred yards, on the east side, which was literally alive with geysers and steamjets. We remained two days in this wonderful basin. The most prominent geysers which we saw in operation we named as follows: 'Old Faithful,' which was farthest up the river on the western bank; 'The Castle' which was a third of a mile below 'Old Faithful;' 'The Giant,' which was a half-mile below 'The Castle;' 'The Grotto,' a short distance below 'The Giant;' then crossing the river, lowest down was the 'Fantail,' and much higher up, nearly opposite 'Old Faithful,' were 'The Giantess' and 'Beehive.' All around the geysers the ground was covered with incrustations and subsilica, and immediately about the vent of most of them the incrustations rose several feet above the surrounding level, assuming grotesque and fanciful shapes."

—WALTER TRUMBALL, *OVERLAND MONTHLY,* JUNE 1871

Anemone Geyser ◀
Beauty Pool ▶

Beehive Geyser ▶

"This morning we were awakened by a fearful, hissing sound, accompanied by the rush of falling water, and, looking out, saw on the other side of the stream a small crater, three feet in height, and with an opening of twenty-six inches diameter, which had scarcely been noticed on the previous day, and was now playing a perpendicular jet to the height of two hundred nineteen feet, with great clouds of steam escaping, and causing the ground to tremble as the heavy body of water fell with tremendous splashes upon the shelly strata below. Huge masses of the rocks were torn from their places and borne away into the river channel. It played thus, steadily, for ten minutes, giving us time to obtain an accurate measurement by triangulation, which resulted as above stated. This crater gave no notice of being a geyser; its appearance and size were altogether insignificant, compared with others."

—G.C. Doane of the General H.D. Washburn-Langford-Doane Expedition, 1870

Beehive Geyser
with rainbow ▶

"'The Beehive'—named for the shape of its mound—was quite small, but threw its water higher than any other geyser we saw. The stream was less than two feet in diameter, and ascended two hundred and twenty feet, from accurate measurement by triangulation. It remained in action only a few moments."

—Walter Trumball, *Overland Monthly*, June 1871

"Upon going into camp we observed a small hot spring that had apparently built itself up about three feet. The water was warm but resting very quietly, and we camped within two hundred yards of it. While we were eating breakfast, this spring, without any warning, threw, as if it were the nozzle of an enormous steam engine, a stream of water into the air two hundred and nineteen feet, and continued doing so for some time, thereby enabling us to measure it, and then suddenly subsided."

—General H.D. Washburn, *Explorations in a New and Wonderful Country*, 1870

Castle Geyser
in Four Moods:

Castle Geyser in
major eruption ▶

Castle Geyser ▶

"Near the bank of the river, and a half a mile below camp, rose on the farther margin of a marshy lake the Castle Crater, the largest formation in the valley. The calcareous knoll on which it stands is forty feet in height, and covers several acres. The crater is built up from its center, with irregular walls of spherical nodules, in forms of wondrous beauty, to a castellated turret, forty feet in height and two hundred feet in circumference at the base. The outer rim, at its summit, is formed in embrasures between large nodules of rock, of the tint of ashes of roses, and in the center is a crater three feet in diameter, bordered and lined with a frostwork of saffron. From a distance it strongly resembles an old feudal tower partially in ruins. This great crater is continually pouring forth steam, the condensation of which keeps the outside walls constantly wet and dripping. The deposit is silver-gray in color, and the structure is wonderful in its massiveness, completion, and exquisite tracery of outline. At the base of the turret lies a large pine log, covered with a nodular and brilliant incrustation to the depth of several inches. The wood of this log is also petrified. The waters of this geyser have burst out in a new place, near the foot of the old crater, flowing a large stream, boiling violently, and diminishing the action of the great vent, yet we saw the latter on one occasion throw water to the perpendicular height of sixty feet, with the escape of heavy volumes of steam. It had doubtless been, when intact, the greatest fountain of them all."

—G.C. Doane of the General H.D. Washburn-Langford-Doane Expedition, 1870

Castle Geyser ▶

"About the crater of 'The Castle' was the largest cone, or mass of incrustations, in the basin. For a hundred yards around, the ground, flooded with subsilica, of glittering whiteness, sloped gradually up to the cone, which itself rose thirty feet, nearly perpendicular. It was quite rugged and efflorescent, and on its outer sides had a number of benches… Its crater, which was irregular in shape, [was] about seven feet, the longest way, by five feet, the shortest. The outside of the mound was nearly round, and not less than thirty feet through at its base. We called it 'The Castle,' on account of its size and commanding appearance. It was in action a short time on the morning after our arrival, but only threw water about thirty feet high. The water did not retain the shape of a column, like that thrown out by 'Old Faithful,' but rather splashed up and slopped over. This geyser did not appear to be doing its best, but only spouted a little in a patronizing way, thinking to surprise us novices sufficiently without any undue exertion on its part."

—Walter Trumball, *Overland Monthly*, June 1871

Castle Geyser in steam phase ◄

"Most of the spring borders are low and daintily scalloped, crenelated, and beaded with sinter pearls; but some of the geyser craters are massive and picturesque, like ruined castles or old burned-out sequoia stumps, and are adorned on a grand scale with outbulging, cauliflower-like formations. From these as centres the silex pavements slope gently away in thin, crusty, overlapping layers, slightly interrupted in some places by low terraces."

—JOHN MUIR, "THE YELLOWSTONE NATIONAL PARK," *THE ATLANTIC MONTHLY*, APRIL 1898

Chromatic Pool, May 2007 ▲

Chromatic Pool and neighboring Beauty Pool share a heating system. Their colors change as water temperature varies, shifting from blue, green, yellow, and orange with hotter water to dark rusty red and brown when the water temperature falls.

Chromatic Pool, May 2008 ▲

Rising water temperatures caused the color shift that occurred between May 2007 and May 2008.

Crested Pool ▲

"Nearby [Castle Geyser, *ed.*], and on the same hillock, is a bluestone spring, with an indented marginal basin, twenty-five feet in diameter; this stands level-full. Its interior lining is of a silver tint, and the water in its perpendicular shaft appears to be of unfathomable depth."

—G.C. DOANE OF THE GENERAL H.D. WASHBURN-LANGFORD-DOANE EXPEDITION, 1870

"Here we found a beautiful spring or well. Raised around it was a border of pure white, carved as if by the hand of a masterwork man, the water pure. Looking down into it one can see the sides white and clear as alabaster, and carved in every conceivable shape...."

—GENERAL H.D. WASHBURN, *EXPLORATIONS IN A NEW AND WONDERFUL COUNTRY,* 1870

Daisy
Geyser ◀

Giantess Geyser crater above bacterial mat ▼
Doublet Pool ▶

Giant Geyser ◄

"A few hundred yards farther down the stream is a crater of flinty rock, in shape resembling a huge shattered horn, broken off half way from its base. It is twelve feet in height, with a solid base; its sides have a curvilinear slope, tagged edges, and its cavity or nozzle is seven feet in diameter. During its quiescent state the boiling water can be seen in its chambers at a depth of forty feet, the action of the steam and water together producing a loud rumbling sound. Near and acting in concert with it are half a dozen smaller craters from two to eight feet in height constantly full of water, and boiling violently from two to six feet into the air. This great geyser played several times while we were in the valley, on one occasion throwing constantly for over three hours a stream of water seven feet in diameter from ninety to two hundred feet perpendicularly. While playing it doubled the size of the Firehole River, running at its maximum about 2,500 inches of water."
—G.C. Doane of the General H.D. Washburn-Langford-Doane Expedition, 1870

"The mound around 'The Giant' was about twelve feet high, and had a piece knocked out of one side of [its, *ed.*] crater, which was shaped like a hollow cylinder, and six feet in diameter. 'The Giant' discharged a column of water, of the same size as its crater, to a height of a hundred feet. It played as if through an immense hose. We thought it deserved to be called 'The Giant,' as it threw out more water than any other geyser which we saw in operation. Its cone was also large, and the water was very hot, as in fact, was the case with the water of all the geysers. The day of our arrival, it was in nearly constant action for about three hours, after which we did not see it again discharge."
—Walter Trumball, *Overland Monthly*, June 1871

Giant Geyser with rainbow ▼

Grand Geyser ◀

"Opposite camp, on the other side of the river, is a high ledge of stalagmite, sloping from the base of the mountain down to the river; numerous small knolls are scattered over its surface. The craters of boiling springs from fifteen to twenty-five feet in diameter; some of these throw water the height of three and four feet. In the summit of this bank of rock is the grand geyser of the world, a well in the strata twenty by twenty-five feet in diametric measurements, the perceptible elevation of the rim being but a few inches, and when quiet having a visible depth of one hundred feet. The edge of the basin is bounded by a heavy fringe of rock, and stalagmite in solid layers is deposited by the overflowing waters. When an eruption is about to occur the basin suddenly fills with boiling water to within a few feet of the surface, then suddenly, with heavy concussions, immense clouds of steam rise to the height of five hundred feet. The whole great body of water, twenty by twenty-five feet, ascends in one gigantic column to the height of ninety feet, and from its apex five great jets shoot up, radiating slightly from each other, to the unparalleled altitude of two hundred fifty feet from the ground. The earth trembles under the descending deluge from this vast fountain, a thousand hissing sounds are heard in the air; rainbows encircle the summits of the jets with a halo of celestial glory. The falling water plows up and bears away the shelly strata, a seething flood pours down the slope and into the river. It is the grandest, the most majestic, and the most terrible fountain in the world. After playing thus for twenty minutes it gradually subsides, the water lowering into the crater out of sight, the steam ceases to escape and all is quiet. This grand geyser played three times in the afternoon, but appears to be irregular in its periods, as we did not see it in eruption again while in the valley. Its waters are of a deep ultramarine color, clear and beautiful. The waving to and fro of the gigantic fountain, when its jets are at their highest, and in a bright sunlight, affords a spectacle of wonder of which any description can give but a feeble idea. Our whole party were wild with enthusiasm; many declared it was three hundred feet in height; but I have kept, in the figures as set down above, within the limits of absolute certainty."

—G.C. Doane of the General H.D. Washburn-Langford-Doane Expedition, 1870

Grand Geyser
with Vent Geyser to the left ◄

Grand Geyser mud ▼

Grotto Geyser's unusual cone ▲

"…a beautiful arched spray, called by us the Grotto, with several apertures…each making so many vents for the water and steam."

—General H.D. Washburn, *Explorations in a New and Wonderful Country*, 1870

"'The Grotto' has two craters, connected on the surface by the incrustations which surround them. We did not ascertain whether there was any subterranean connection between them. We did not observe both craters discharge at the same time, but one began when the other ceased. Neither was in action for more than an hour. A solid stream was thrown up more than sixty feet; that from the larger crater being about five feet in diameter, and that from the smaller one not more than three feet. The larger mound of incrustations was about ten feet high, and twenty feet through at the base…. The smaller mound was not more than five feet high, and shaped like a haycock, with a portion of the top knocked off. The two mounds were about twenty feet apart, and connected by a ridge, or neck of incrustations, two feet high. 'The Grotto' was about a hundred yards from the river."

—Walter Trumball, *Overland Monthly*, June 1871

Heart Spring ▲

Morning Glory Pool ▲
Lion Geyser Group ◀

Oblong Geyser and Chromatic Pool ▲
Riverside Geyser ▶

Old Faithful ▶

"Near the head of the valley, immediately after crossing to the south side of the [Firehole, *ed.*] river, we came to one of the geysers, which was at the time throwing water, with a loud hissing sound, to the height of one hundred twenty-five feet. In a few minutes the eruption ceased, and we were enabled to approach the crater. This had originally been a crack or fissure in the calcareous ledge, the seam of which could be traced by minute vents a distance of sixty feet, but was now closed up by deposits from the water to an opening seven feet long by three feet wide in the center, from which the steam escaped with a loud, rushing sound. The hillock formed by the spring is forty feet in height, and its base covers about four acres. Near the crater, and as far as its irruptive waters reach, the character of the deposit is very peculiar. Close around the opening are built up walls, eight feet in height, of spherical nodules, from six inches to three feet in diameter. These, in turn, are covered on the surface with minute globules of calcareous stalagmite, incrusted with a thin glazing of silica. The rock, at a distance, appears the color of ashes of roses, but near at hand shows a metallic gray, with pink and yellow margins of the utmost delicacy. Being constantly wet, the colors are brilliant beyond description. Sloping gently from this rim of the crater in every direction, the rocks are full of cavities, in successive terraces, forming little pools, with margins of silica the color of silver, the cavities being irregular shape, constantly full of hot water, and precipitating delicate coral-like beads of a bright saffron. These cavities are also fringed with rock around the edges, in meshes as delicate as the finest lace. Diminutive yellow columns rise from their depths, capped with small tablets of rock, and resembling flowers growing in the water. Some of them are filled with oval pebbles of a brilliant white color, and others with a yellow frostwork which builds up gradually in solid stalagmites.

Receding still further from the crater, the cavities become gradually larger, and the water cooler, causing changes in the brilliant colorings, and also in the formations of the deposits. These become calcareous spar, of a white or slate color, and occasionally variegated. The water of the geyser is colorless, tasteless, and without odor. The deposits are apparently as delicate as the down on the butterfly's wing, both in texture and coloring, yet are firm and solid beneath the tread. Those who have seen stage representations of 'Aladdin's Cave,' and the 'Home of the Dragon Fly,' as produced in a first-class theater, can form an idea of the wonderful coloring, but not of the intricate frostwork, of this fairy-like, yet solid mound of rock, growing up amid clouds of steam and showers of boiling water.... The beauty of the scene takes away one's breath. It is overpowering, transcending the visions of the Moslem's Paradise. The earth affords not its equal. It is the most lovely inanimate object in existence. The period of this geyser is fifty minutes. First an increased rush of steam comes forth, followed instantly by a rising jet of water, which attains, by increased impulsions, to the height of one hundred twenty-five feet, escaping with a wild, hissing sound, while great volumes of steam rise up to an altitude of five hundred feet from the crater. Rainbows play around the tremendous fountain, the waters of which fall about the basin in showers of brilliance, then rush steaming down the slopes to the river. After a continuous action for a space of five minutes, the jet lowers convulsively by degrees, the waters finally disappear, and only a current of steam pours forth from the crater. When we consider that it plays through an aperture seven by three feet in measurement, an idea can be formed of the vast quantity of water ejected by this great natural fountain."

—G.C. DOANE OF THE GENERAL H.D. WASHBURN-LANGFORD-DOANE EXPEDITION, 1870

"After eating our suppers we started out on a tour of inspection. Old Faithful was the first to secure our attention. This wonderful geyser gives an exhibition of its strength every sixty-five minutes with astonishing regularity. Through winter and summer, day and night, year in and year out, it is unerringly 'on time.' So regular are its eruptions that the name of 'Old Faithful' is certainly no misnomer. Its eruptions begin with a few spasmodic spurts, which throw the water fully fifteen feet into the air. These are followed a few minutes later by a column of boiling water and steam several feet in diameter, which is thrown to a height of one hundred and fifty to two hundred and fifty feet. For several minutes this column remains, when it gradually recedes and lies dormant for sixty-five minutes. Then the phenomena is repeated."

—EDWARD S. PARKINSON, *WONDERLAND; OR, TWELVE WEEKS IN AND OUT OF THE UNITED STATES,* 1894

Sawmill
Geyser ▶

Upper Geyser Basin ▶

"I have now described seven of the largest geysers seen in the Firehole Basin, and the description falls far short of the reality. To do justice to the subject would require a volume. The geysers of Iceland sink to insignificance beside them; they are above the reach of comparison. We could not distinguish, on every occasion, the geysers from the other hot springs, except by seeing them play, and doubtless there are many besides in the valley of great size, which we saw when quiet, and classed as boiling springs. They all vary in times, force, deposits, and colors of water. The number of springs of all kinds in the valley is not less than fifteen hundred; and, with the exception of Bluestone Springs, scarcely any two are exactly alike. Taken as an aggregate, the Firehole Basin surpasses all other great wonders of the continent. It produces an effect on the mind of the beholder utterly staggering and overpowering. During the night we were several times awakened by the rush of steam and the hissing of the waters, as the restless geysers spouted forth in the darkness. A constant rumbling, as of machinery in labor, filled the air, which was damp and warm throughout the night."

—G.C. Doane of the General H.D. Washburn-Langford-Doane Expedition, 1870

WEST THUMB GEYSER BASIN

"I rode around the head of the lake to the steam jets visible from camp; this was the largest system we had yet seen, located at the extreme point of the most westerly arm of the lake, and on a gentle slope, reaching along the shore for a mile, and extending back into the woods for the same distance; this system embraced every variety of hot water and mud springs seen thus far on the route, with many other heretofore unseen. Four hundred yards from the lakeshore is a basin of mud having a bright pink color; this is a system of itself, being seventy feet in diameter, and projecting thick mud through small craters of a conical shape around the edge of the basin, while the center is one seething mass. The deposit speedily hardens into a firm, laminated clay stone, of beautiful texture, though the brilliant pink color fades to a chalky white. Near and around this basin are a dozen springs, from six to twenty-five feet across, boiling muddy water of paint-like consistency, in colors varying from a pure white to a dark yellow; them come several flowing springs, from ten to fifty feet in diameter, of clear, hot water, the basins and channels of which were lined with deposits of red, green, yellow, and black, giving them an appearance of gorgeous splendor; these deposits were too friable to preserve, crumbling at the touch. The bright colors were on the surface of the rock only, not extending to its interior. Below these were several large craters of bluish water impregnated with sulphate of copper; these boiled to the height of two feet in the center and flowed large streams of water; their rims were raised a few inches, in a delicate rocky margin of a fringe-like appearance, deposited from the water. Beyond these are two lakes of purple water, hot, but not boiling; these give deposits of great delicacy of coloring. Nearby are two more bluestone springs, the largest we have yet seen; one, thirty by forty feet and of temperature 173 degrees F, flows a stream into the other one about seventy feet distant, and six feet lower; this latter spring is forty by seventy-five feet, temperature 183 degrees F; a stream of one hundred inches of water flows from it. The craters of these springs are of calcareous stalagmite, and lined with a silvery white deposit which illuminates, by reflection, the interior an immense depth; both crates have perpendicular but irregular walls, and the distance to which objects are visible down in their deep abysses is truly wonderful. No figure of imagination, no description of enchantment, can equal in imagery the vista of these great basins. West of these is a group, of clear, hot water, which surpass them all for singularity, though not in beauty; these are basins of different sizes and unknown depths, in which float what appear to be raw bullock-hides as they look in a tanner's vat, waving sluggishly about with every undulation of the water; the resemblance is complete. On examination the leathery substance proves to be a fragile texture, something like the vegetable scum in stagnant pools, ("and yet it is not vegetable.") with brilliant colors of red, yellow, green, and black, on the shaded side. It is easily torn and could not be preserved, unless indeed by pressure, like rose leaves; it has the thickness and flabbiness of rawhide, and is quite heavy when wet. Digging down into the basins, I found that this singular substance filled the whole depth, layer upon layer being deposited; and stranger than all, the lower strata were solidified, turning to pure, finely-grained sheets of alabaster, specimens of which I brought in.

"On the margin of the lake is a double row of calcareous springs at the boiling point, (here 185 degrees F,) which do not flow, except at intervals. These build up craters of solid limestone, from five to twenty feet in height; many of these stand in the waters of the lake, and several are partially broken away by the erosive action of its waves. There are two flowing ones, with low craters from twenty to thirty feet in diameter, which run as much as fifty inches of boiling water each. Of these, the walls of the craters are visible to a great depth, inclining at a sharp angle under the bed of the lake, and separated from it by thin barriers of shelving rock. All along the shore, for a mile, runs a terrace of calcareous stalagmite, in a deposit of from twenty to fifty feet in depth, the edges of which are worn to a bluff bank by the action of the waters. This stratum has been deposited by the mingled streams of mineral waters of every sort, which flow from the springs above and flood its whole surface. The rock is stained with variegated colors, which speedily fade, but specimens obtained from the lower beds, and bleached in the lake, are the purest of alabaster. Scattered over the surface of this terrace are masses of calcareous tufa, which, when dried, will float in water. Not less than one thousand inches of hot water flow into the lake at this point, and numberless jets can be seen boiling up far out in its basin. In this enumeration I have described but a few of the largest springs; there are hundreds of them, including vapor vents, mud spouts, and still caldrons. They are scattered through the woods in such numbers as to require the utmost care to prevent stumbling into them at every turn. Occasionally this anomaly is seen, of two springs, at different levels, both boiling violently; one pours a large and constant stream into the other,

yet the former does not diminish, nor does the latter fill up and overflow. Most of the springs, however, seem to be independent of each other and to come form immense depths, having different levels at the surface, different temperatures, and pulsations; seldom are found the waters and deposits of any two exactly alike. It is impossible to adequately describe, and utterly impossible to realize from any description, more than a faint idea of the beauties and wonders of this group."

—G.C. DOANE OF THE GENERAL H.D. WASHBURN-LANGFORD-DOANE EXPEDITION, 1870

Seismograph and Bluebell Pools ▼

Abyss Pool ▲

Abyss Pool's walls, "coral-like in formation and singular in shape, tinted by the water's color, are surely good representations of fairy palaces."

—W.W. WYLIE, *YELLOWSTONE*, 1882

Bacterial mats ▲

"Our last camp on the lake was near the extremity of the southwest arm. Close by us was a collection of warm springs —the largest, most numerous, varied, and peculiar which we had then discovered. Several were from fifty to eighty feet in length, by from twenty to fifty in width. The water was generally clear, and of great depth. All were hot, but of different temperatures. Around the larger ones the ground was marshy, and largely composed of a reddish earth, which looked like wet brickdust. A number of hot streams flowed from these springs into the lake. The lakeshore was covered with subsilica, broken into small pieces, and washed smooth by the action of the waves. Many of these pieces were pure and white as alabaster."

—WALTER TRUMBALL, *OVERLAND MONTHLY*, JUNE 1871

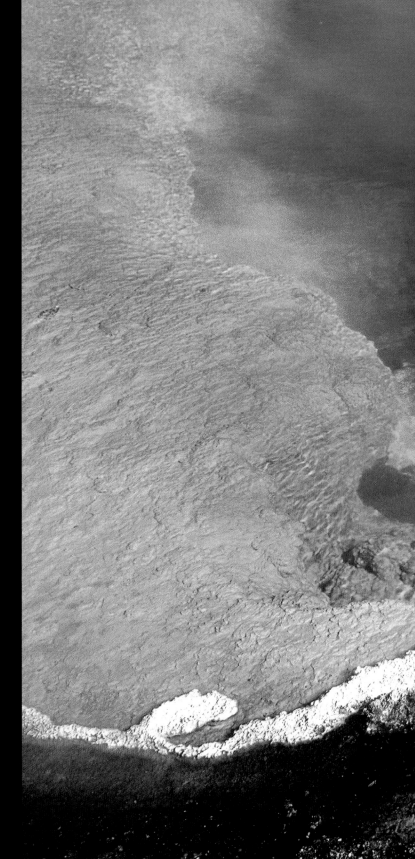

Black Pool ▲
Black Pool detail ▶

Lakeshore Geyser ▼

"Many of the smaller springs were mud springs, boiling and spluttering incessantly. These were generally a few feet below the surface, and encased in clay banks. They emitted a strong sulphurous smell, which rendered a close examination rather disagreeable. Several springs were in solid rock, within a few feet of the lakeshore. Some of them extended far out underneath the lake, with which, however, they had no connection. The lake water was quite cold, and that of these springs exceedingly hot. They were remarkably clear, and the eye could penetrate a hundred feet into their depths, which to the human vision appeared bottomless."

—WALTER TRUMBALL, *OVERLAND MONTHLY*, JUNE 1871

Fishing Cone ▼

"A gentleman [Cornelius Hedges, *ed.*] was fishing from
one of the narrow isthmuses, or shelves of rock, which
divided one of these hot springs from the [Yellowstone,
ed.] lake, when, swinging a trout ashore, it accidentally
got off the hook and fell into the spring. For a moment
it darted about with wonderful rapidity, as if seeking an
outlet. Then it came to the top, dead, and literally boiled."

—WALTER TRUMBALL, *OVERLAND MONTHLY,* JUNE 1871

West Thumb Geyser Basin ◄

"There were several hundred springs here, varying in size from miniature fountains to pools or wells seventy-five feet in diameter and of great depth. The water had a pale violet tinge, and was very clear, enabling us to discern small objects fifty or sixty feet below the surface. In some of these, vast openings led off at the side; and as the slanting rays of the sun lit up these deep caverns, we could see the rocks hanging from their roofs, their water-worn sides and rocky floors, almost as plainly as if we had been traversing their silent chambers…. At the water's edge, along the lakeshore, there were several mounds of solid stone, on the top of each of which was a small basin with a perforated bottom; these also overflowed at times, and the hot water trickled down on every side. Thus, by the slow process of precipitation, through the countless lapse of ages, these stone monuments have been formed. A small cluster of mud springs nearby claimed our attention. They were like hollow truncated cones and oblong mounds, three or four feet in height. These were filled with mud, resembling thick paint of the finest quality, differing in color, from pure white to the various shades of yellow, pink, red and violet. Some of these boiling pots were less than a foot in diameter. The mud in them would slowly rise and fall as the bubbles of escaping steam, following one after the other, would burst upon the surface. During the afternoon, they threw mud to the height of fifteen feet for a few minutes, and then settled back to their former quietude."

—David Folsom of the Folsom-Cook-Peterson Expedition, 1869

New growth near South Entrance ▲

Yellowstone Lake ◀

"Lake Yellowstone is a lonely, but lovely inland sea, everywhere surrounded by 'forests primeval,' and nestled in the bosom of the Rocky Mountains. Its shape resembles the broad hand.… The palm of the hand represents the main body, or north part, of the lake. The fingers and thumb, spread to their utmost extent —the thumb and little finger being much the longest —represent inlets indenting the south shore, and stretching inland, as if to wash away the Rocky Mountains. Between these inlets project high, rocky promontories, covered with dense timber. The largest stream flows into the lake at its upper end, or the extreme southeast corner. This stream is really the Yellowstone River, which, for a distance of thirty miles, has an average width of over fifteen miles. This enlargement constitutes the lake, which, after being augmented by several smaller streams, narrows down to the width of an eighth of a mile, and flows northward toward the great falls. The mood of the lake is ever changing; the character of its shore is ever varying. At one moment, it is placid and glassy as a calm summer's sea; at the next, 'it breaks into dimples, and laughs in the sun.' Half an hour later, beneath a stormy sky, its waters may be broken and lashed into an angry and dangerous sea, like the short, choppy waves which rise in storms on Lake Erie and Lake Michigan. Where we first saw it, it had a glittering beach of gray and rock-crystal sand, but as we continued around it, we found rocky and muddy shores, gravel beaches —on which several varieties of chalcedony were profusely scattered —and hot springs in abundance."

—Walter Trumball, *Overland Monthly,* June 1871

"Passing through many a mile of pine and spruce woods, toward the centre of the park you come to the famous Yellowstone Lake. It is about twenty miles long and fifteen wide, and lies at a height of nearly eight thousand feet above the level of the sea, amid dense black forests and snowy mountains. Around its winding, wavering shores, closely forested and picturesquely varied with promontories and bays, the distance is more than one hundred miles. It is not very deep, only from two hundred to three hundred feet, and contains less water than the celebrated Lake Tahoe of the California Sierra, which is nearly the same size, lies at a height of sixty-four hundred feet, and is over sixteen hundred feet deep. But no other lake in North America of equal area lies so high as the Yellowstone, or gives birth to so noble a river. The terraces around its shores show that at the close of the glacial period its surface was about one hundred sixty feet higher than it is now, and its area nearly twice as great.

"In calm weather it is a magnificent mirror for the woods and mountains and sky, now pattered with hail and rain, now roughened with sudden storms that send waves to fringe the shores and wash its border of gravel and sand. The Absaroka Mountains and the Wind River Plateau on the east and south pour their gathered waters into it, and the river issues from the north side in a broad, smooth, stately current, silently gliding with such serene majesty that one fancies it knows the vast journey of four thousand miles that lies before it, and the work it has to do."

—John Muir, "The Yellowstone National Park," *The Atlantic Monthly,* April 1898

INDEX OF THERMAL FEATURES

Mud Volcano detail ▲